I Brake for Clouds

A Cloud Watchers Book

Dian Cunningham Parrotta

RESOURCE *Publications* · Eugene, Oregon

I BRAKE FOR CLOUDS
A Cloud Watchers Book

Resource Publications
An Imprint of Wipf and Stock Publishers
199 W. 8th Ave., Suite 3
Eugene, OR 97401

www.wipfandstock.com

PAPERBACK ISBN: 978-1-7252-8323-7
HARDCOVER ISBN: 978-1-7252-8324-4
EBOOK ISBN: 978-1-7252-8325-1

Manufactured in the U.S.A.   08/28/20

I Brake for Clouds

Dedicated to Gavin Pretor-Pinney,
founder of The Cloud Appreciation Society
www.cloudappreciationsociety.org/collecting

Unsplash: The internet's source of freely-usable images.
Powered by creators everywhere

and to all our children,
who are our youngest scientists
cloud physicists(!)
and to all our future weather anchors,
artists, teachers,
story tellers and
poets~

photo by armand-khoury-Ba611mAzl-k-unsplash.jpg

Set their feet on the first rung of a ladder,
the top of which sticks through the sky

—ROBERT FROST

Contents

fog in the troposphere~photo by Arthur aldyrkhanov@aldyrkhanov

Introduction

CLOUD WATCHING IS A great hobby. Maybe you have already seen a floating rooster or a slow floating turtle? I saw my dog Simon, a big white English Bull dog floating up in the sky and that made me smile. Do you know when you spot things out of designs there is a special name you call that. When you can see a face in the moon or see images inside of the clouds that's called pareidolia.

Pareidolia is when you can see faces and images inside of something, well, like what you see when you look up at the floating clouds. Look up into the sky. See if you can see things that are moving by. You might see a cat or a dinosaur. You might see a frog or a horse or a dragon with big sharp teeth. Go find a grassy spot in your yard or at a park and yes, lie down and look up right into the sky.

You must be thinking just how high up are the clouds you watch as they float by above so elegantly wafting in the breeze. *Clouds are named on how they are shaped and how high or low they drift inside the troposphere.*

Well it all starts in the *Troposphere where your two feet are touching the grass and goes up to 10,000 to 60,000 feet like up to 12 miles above your head. Look up. The air closest to the Earth is warmer, which means the higher you go upwards, the colder it is.*

The Troposphere is one of the five layers of the Earth's atmosphere, and the others are called stratosphere, mesosphere, thermosphere and exosphere. There are high-level clouds way high in the troposphere, these clouds and their names are cirrus clouds and they look like delicate threads of wispy hair. They are made of ice crystals. Then there are clouds that are middle-level and there are low-level clouds too. I think you need to research the names of these following kinds of clouds. Maybe you can make a painting of each kind of cloud and where they are located inside of the troposphere!

High clouds include cirrus, cirrocumulus, and cirrostratus

Middle clouds include altocumulus and altostratus

Low clouds include cumulus, stratus, and stratocumulus

How about make a big poster of our Earth's atmosphere? I wonder how you will draw our atmosphere, or will you paint it? I guess you could even write atmosphere poetry! That is what I am going to do here in this cloud watching book. Will you join me? I am a big fan of kid-friendly browsers and these following sites are a quick, safe spots to go to do some cloud research:

www.kidskonnect.com/science/troposphere

www.nationalgeographic.com

Hey, you can also become a member of the Cloud Appreciation Society by visiting www.cloudappreciationsociety.org. I am a proud member and cannot tell you what fun it is to belong to a community that loves clouds as much as I do. This website shares a lot of information on photographing clouds and they have gallery where you can post your awesome cloud photos and cloud poetry!

Clouds are found almost all the time in the troposphere because that is where all the water and dust particles stay though you can find an occasional thin blankets of clouds above the troposphere. You do know clouds are made of water! You would not be able to count the millions and trillions of water droplets or bits of frozen water, called ice crystals, that are inside of each floating cloud. Wouldn't it be fun to swim inside of a white puffy ball cloud?

Be a cloud watcher and see their odd and delightful shapes. Part of the fun is to just stare into the endless universe. I know you will come up with great stories, paintings and poems on what you see and before you know it you will want to know more about clouds and become hooked on weather! If you are already interested in finding out about the weather, you might consider joining the American Meteorological Society. Anyone who is interested can join at www.ametsoc.org. You might be a future weather anchor!

I have three favorite cloud books I want to share with you. The first book is titled, *The Book of Clouds*, written by John Day, a doctor of cloud physics and a professor of meteorology. The other two cloud books are titled: *The Cloud Collector's Handbook* and *The Cloud a Day book* which contains an 365 cloudscape skies that will make you appreciate paying more of your attention to the clouds you see when you look up and which is why Gavin Pretor-Pinney, the founder of The Cloud Appreciation Society, published these two books, thinking about you all the while. I have my own copies and love these awesome cloud books. They are both helpful in introducing the reader to clouds and serves as a great resource for those of us who just love to have them in our libraries.

Low Cloud Poetry

photo by david-monje-77Aw8rM9KGg-unsplash.jpg

photo by todd-steitle-exnadmin-asc-unsplash.jpg

you illuminate

It's so easy
to forget you
live in the sky
and not beneath
among snowy white
owl clouds floating
ground nesters' dreams
like you are
the black sunset
you lie down
with the moon
inside the clouds
the deciduous trees
then the evergreens
in your heights
a thin below
the sun thickens
near your horizon
coronal colors pass
right through you
like a cloud

fog photo by Fabrizio-conti-jfukGbidyKE-unsplash.jpg

Fog

a kind of cloud,
a flat, a hazy,
featureless
quiet as grass
hoovering
with smoky grays
drifting troubadours
trabairitz dressed in veils
in soft wools and linens
move along
a smoke-white stratus'
a dusty light
travelling
alongside the road
meandering
celestial waters
the sky slips
dips counterclockwise
like blind fish

photo by ricardo-gomez-angel on unsplash

Can Fog?

Does the fog, the lowest forming of all the cloud types, play with the frogs by hiding the pond inside of its slate gray mist? Hear the croaking by the slippery elm where the tadpoles, the little polliwogs, flutter in algae in the rush and sedge near the spider lily hidden under creeping branches, rooting at the nodes near the growing marsh marigold and moss—spongy ground a bog aww sonorous to hear harmonious ribbits nothing like their croaks' husky snoring sounds' all in one voice under their throats those sighing patterns of serenade heard from the hidden wetland swathed in cloudy gray a pearly undertone the fog so sunken resembling a lazy shallow-Stratus

photo by debby-hudson-u73tEFydlGk-unsplash.jpg

cumulus humilis

above the sunward slope of Mount Hood Mountain, Oregon's tallest peak, heated by the rising sun with those thermals of rushing air causing a little puff of a very small convection cloud floating puffy flattened wider than its tall a shape above the atmospheric phenomena and colors of a trillium twilight, like with mineral paints and there in the foliage with those native large-flowering three-petal flowers streaked with maroon. ovate and wavy-edged this late spring June this leaf whorl each sprouting a single bloom. Floating above the veitch's dark violet blue globe thistle iridescent glow clump 4 feet tall with its spiny leaves with butterflies & bees & hummingbirds with bearded irises with more leaves delicate things like on water-color drawings. This fair-weather cloud floating high above colorful kayak canoes by the lakeside beaches, the campsites with watchful heaps of creek stones looking up towards the sky, the cottages with their rocking chairs, the wicker and swings viewing this morning's small common cloud, a cumulus humilis, as it dissipates moving along with the wind

April 24, 2020 / In Cloud Poetry Homepage The Cloud Appreciation Society,
photo by eugenia guetogomez

fair-weather cumulus

Cumulus-clouds are those clouds we drew in first- grade classrooms
using Elmer's glue and white cotton ball puffs.
Cumulus come detached in heaps and tons thick and bulky huge
like angel statues white tussocks of cloud tons
floating cascading candy tufts and an airy pavlova topped with whipped cream.
White perennials in bloom luxuriant snowy flower farms' land views
with bleached roses protruding inner petals
their edges neatly penciled in with white.
The Zinnias, the giant magnolia flower,
the coneflowers, the hydrangeas, hyacinths, gardenias and white orchids,
the daylilies oh their bundles of bloom.
The iris, and those white peonies and other such sun perennial varieties
or look at those floating floppy polar bears roaming over there
thick detached tongues of icebergs and glaciers iced meadows moving
a subdued silence and do you see Bumble the abominable snow man?

photo by alex-parkes on unsplash

All Earth Basks in the Sunshine

the minutes
deferred
between the mouthfuls of sunshine
in blue sky
and the swelling pieces of cumulus clouds
thickens floating by
an overcast
unfriendly
then the sun's brilliance
parades
once again

Changes-sprawling
multi-level clouds forming

as white as the neighbors' sabbath fish
dish made from a poached mixture of ground deboned gefilte fish
with cut loose the tail off the fish   flapping
the cirrus wispy whites
of brushstrokes thin ringlets
or curling long strands
or those stratus clouds fuzzy
gray blankets my Irish grandpa john kept on all beds
a winter must haves in Saugerties
and the cumulus fluffy cotton balls
fluffy floating but can change into multi-level gray
often darker even jet-black ragged
stretched to its edges
scudding in
with dim imposing undersides
tumbling
nimbus amorphous
an ominous rain-hail—sleet-snow producing
slashing
severe winds,
chaotic air
tornadoes must reach the ground
otherwise your talking funnel or wall clouds
but tornadoes form from a cut off the base
underneath it
off of the parent cloud
free blowing rotating debris & dust
untamed
cyclonic winds of pipe shapes
rope-like thin
spinning

from the geometry of the shadow

clouds floating in a Catskill Mountain Creek tributary of the Hudson River draining the East-central mountains of the U.S. State of New York in Saugerties where my grandpa john and grandma gee bee used to live behind a running water creek beneath those Fair-weather Cumulus clouds and up those stepping-stone stairs, out of stuck slate slabs and stones with snakes that floating in the deep side of the creek looking like the Blackthorn short shillelaghos, those black Irish walking sticks, dark skinned serpents drifting and there those boulders sun dried and creek rocks & fish are eating large horse flies on the surfaces of fallen low clouds floating, white breakfast plates, among leaves and wet river stones with rainbow-knotted sprays splashing mossy homes of crayfish. Look at the minnows in the streams' banks the fallfish & the creeks' chubs and the long-legged water striders, those water skeeters or skooters skate on top of still dimpling surfaces forces interfaces dragging geometric leg shadows' locomotions' of the silvery tensions on water

starlings photo by james-wains coat on unsplash

against a cloudy winter's starling sky

at a moments' notice on the edge with twisting spectacle changes in directions of a swooping into that unpredictability of their intricately coordinated patterns those eerier flocks of hundreds of thousands of starlings fly in fast-moving cloud formations through ascent and push forming funnels into a flanking line with a velum edge of a thin layer of semilunar shapes collapse into a quick shift with momentum on a wave suggestively a Hitchcock-dark a supernatural shapeshifting with fantastical speed causing a collision between air earth waves' swell seismic hums that nobody hears a murmuration that swooping mass they gather over their roosting sites preferring urban artificial structures on power lines, telephone wires or on a monumental mass or tapering towers or on pylons keeping a closeness a warm cozy at night

black lives matter photo by emir.parrotta@gmail.com

a photo by emir

emir took this photograph in Madrid
still hear billy singing those blues from the clouded sky there up there those
clouds in the sky that white cloud floating above Madrid's metro SOL Square.
Can you see a pale pink granite statue centerpiece cloud joining thousands
of people at an anti-racism march outside the United States embassy in
the Spanish capital, in Serrano street in Puerta del Sol ? "*We are one!*" they
shout and chant holding signs *I can't Breathe* protestors outside thousands
with social distancing the two-meter limits of coronavirus shouting slogans
while the cumulus George Floyd frames a message a black couple clenched
in a hug on a stand with loud audible cries of "Madrid will be the tomb of
racism" echoes of a Spanish Civil War against fascism villainous enemies
dressed in fine pearls, blazers, and sweater vests, chinos, with the girls with
the super-straight hair channeling their politics into their wardrobes with
those so learning right make you what you are across the sea, earth, sky, it is
now the beginning of a new spring of *no more strange fruits will sway from
the poplar trees* billy sings

Middle Cloud Poems

altostratus clouds

uninteresting a dull grey sheet cloud a large rectangular piece of old cotton mattress cover sky featureless those boring thin fabric clouds choppy and turbulent unless spotted under the fiery lights from a low sunrise/sunset illuminating those slips in ripples shine crimson golden bolides' white pink-colored cloudy sea small slivers of emerald green pond shimmering billowy upside-down ocean surfaces windy blows like the stuff of Sci-fi fantasy currents moving clockwise patterns sky's ceilings an ocean surface water silky in motion riptides contrasting eerie orange cast in twilight colors alluring altostratus' aerosols moments dramatics captured in slow or fast-moving videos and in landscape photography

anvil cloud photo by martin vysoundil on unsplash

was once under a floating anvil cloud

in the Catskill Mountains' valleys through landscapes with ridges with roll-ing small creeks full of stones with black bears, bobcats we didn't ever see but heard those cougars howling and saw long snakes   like floating black poles in the creek and the many plants and small green leprechauns with their pots full of gold telling us our grandpa's wrought iron from his workshop shed by the barn's gone-went up floating in clouds clamoring up darkness so I had bet then my Grandma Tessy who was in Brooklyn alone in fear afraid all by herself from the sky's ragged undersides of that floating cumulonimbus storm cloud so up high. We all sat on my grandpa's long Saugerties wood front porch cracking walnuts under rocking chairs back and forth with little chubby sister in high yellow boots holding her pink plastic bottle of bubbles blowing from her wand rain pouring outta broken gutters down pouring from the porch with smells of musty barky of dry earth pungent zings of petrichor, ozone, and geosmin scents like the smell of rain water falling on thirsty soil and on hot stone like those fluids that flow in the veins of Greek gods with wet-leaves-soaked smells of beetroot organic—fragrances refreshing whiffs of earth with rain from the cumulo-nimbus storm cloud the big D of clouds thunderheads of darkening gloom fussing raindrops down
the intensity of the winds' *sturm und drang*
howling lightning bolts' flare-ups
broken off from rainclouds
flicker flaps of flashes—a blood thirsty enduring
above tall vertically dark 10 miles high hoo-ha
a heavy dense fluctuating meteorite—black—hovering
block of metal infinitely inflexible, immovable
like caste steel flat head top flying like a bitter hungry falcon bird with its sharp talon and beak
in air undulating
a motion
a firm-floating with winds picking up severe weather looms

a kerfuffle   moving quickly with a flash
flooding fury fermenting a chaos
ferocity flowing dark lumbering's
the harbinger of heavy showers,
thunderstorm twisters
tornadoes—violently rotating columns
—funnel clouds
the vortex of wind
rapidly rotating narrow columns of air with windspeed 300mph
can happen any time of year
"Dorothy! Dorothy!" my big brother yells out and we all run back
into the foyer with wind tearing
the rocky chairs jerk writhe with wind
a long lengthy rocking chairs shuddering

rain falling in puddle photo by alex-dukhanov on unsplash

Ekphrasis poem tribute to Hiroshige

and that famous raining nimbostratus cloud—a dull drab depressing like a featureless a thick grey a lingering a sudden shower a drizzling lots- of- then a down pour drench. Look at the murky block out the sun that famous raining nimbostratus, dim miserable a multi-level cloud, a wet black blanket, featureless in the sky—black across the top of Hiroshige sudden violent summer rain storm prolonged and steady precipitation those sprays over Shin-Ohashi Bridge & Atake,in the ukiyo-e genre . . . from One Hundred Famous views of Edo (1857) with persistent narrow fine counterpart lines a thin persistent angular rainfall flattened a spreading out dark and a solitary boatman poling his raft past pretty pink blossoms of delicate flowers ferrying past blooming cherry trees on the river downstream passing these delightful intricacies and is there anything more lovelier?

& with migrants of geese winging V-shaped patterns these harbingers of springtime.

Then there that adventurous outdoorsman now seeking shelter and those six people crossing the bridge casing under hats, mats and umbrellas a windy wood block print that filtered through Vincent Van Gogh's eyes on a Japanese print with a variant a kind of interlacing colorful, impressionist-style paint brush strokes and replacing color bracing wide ranging textural qualities but keeping true to the Ando Hiroshige's original motif but to his bold use of more color like used in his vibrant reds in his Poppies, those pint clouds in the turquoise sky that Blossoming almond Tree and the yellows, orange, and green leaves twirl along the branches in his famous The Mulberry Tree so happy with his paintbox he had there he wrote and said so in his letter to his brother Theo.

bear photo by oxana-lyashenko on unsplash

the changing Kermode Bear Clouds

there is a spirit bear a rare American black bear in the sky floating heaps of fur detached from the others these fair weather clouds with five sheep grazing in a sky pasture swelling cumulus medium clouds detached with small cloud fragments coasting by—defined of shapes and outlines against the cloudless spaces gently descending air stable and stratified horizontal movements of irregularly shaped blob globules of clouds fluctuating shapes as parts of the cloud evaporates when those black bear clouds is pale. The First Nations communities call this white cloud bear moskgm'ol~~ 'white bear' sacred animal cloud creating a wild precious skyscape with those meek-cud-chewing-wool-covered-soft-curly-hair- baa-baaaa sheep clouds into a one fish two fish blow fish blow up puffers white and cream helium balloons with tiny fins with small tube-shaped lips and mouths slowly disseminate upwardly developing into Cumulus congestus growing into a fierce cumulonimbus storm clouds like black bears enormous dark covering the whole sky growing over ten miles high now the king of clouds producing thunder and lightning stormy

duck Photo by julie adams on unsplash

altocumulus, stratocumulus clouds

makes for exciting time watching the sky eider clouds handsomeness adult males' dud'ed in breading plumage wooly wooly famously thick soft down deep blue white dash-like stripes and spots ducks ducks in a mix blend of cumulus and stratocumulus cloud a most closer to the ground a low-altitude, and somewhat conjoined heaps of cloud raft a demonstration of eider males resting on frazil freeze ice floes with white dreams courting hen queens quack quack off a wintery waterfowling coast all ducks in a row like calm floating but you can't see *their feet daddling like the dickens* underneath rising turret formations or castellanus' wooly locks all in many different shapes and sizes forming into smooth lens shapes then blankets with sac like features like condensed resembling more than any 10 main clouds' dramatic changing now inna volutus cloud but bets those resting short necks swimming and diving 80 feet under to feed on crustaceans, mollusks, & other prey meets a cloud resembling octopuses arm roll swell squishy tentacles when the dark skies reel in long, horizontal tubes detached and so ominous-looking

Midlevel Alto Stratus Clouds

I can see gray featureless splays two-centered grey circle halos, the translucidus, thin enough to show the outline of the moon come form and break on sky shorelines, the sea foam forms white altrostratus curtains of cloud-cotton sheets from beneath like silhouettes of Japanese paper walls giving umbrage like shadows cast by big tall trees, those higher clouds are hidden from view, mid-level altocumulus udulatos, casting a penumbra onto a shallow layer of alto stratus below a pale overcast a translucent umbrella diffuses spreading the light embraces gracefully billowing glowing circles around the moon dog curtains draw across pieces of ground glass thickening membranes. The altostratus rains are on their way.

High Clouds

cloud sweepers

Precipitating those heaps of cumulonimbus clouds 25,000feet up and
higher tons of light
shower
fall from clouds'
mounds and layers
with mists or drizzles tickling tops
of the bamboo leaves in my yard
growing in many-stemmed,and cane-like clumps
up into the sky
with swishing
broom tops
sweeps the clouds that float by

fine lines of cirrus

the flip side of looking through the ocean surface up into the atmosphere where a mysterious veil of gossamer-like clouds dangle far 50 miles up above work in reverse like a mind rewind you got the clouds up and the ocean waves down but it's this thing that happens in the highest clouds on Earth in the noctilucent clouds forming from water-vapor freezes those floating specks of meteor dust-spray layers of faint a faded though floodlit up its silver blues in the twilights to about two hours after sunset or before sunrise *the sun's* brilliance of *the* lower atmosphere brings on this showy sky and the ocean's got its zones too from the surface to extremes where the sunlight can't penetrate those deep the bottom's hadalpelagic sub-oceanic trenches of the underworld unseen where sometimes vengeful a bad-tempered god of the sea, the Brother of Zeus, god of all gods, and brother of Hades, god of the dead and ruler of the underworld—oh, Poseidon controls sea monsters and makes the earth shake and those earthquakes rewinding into violent space quakes, starquakes shake, awakens moonquakes and asteroid quakes seismic tremors rocking wild respectively a million-miles-per-hour a tempestuous weight a turbulent wind shining

high cirrocumulus cloud sky

And the cirrocumulus clouds are part of the high cloud group these look like the scales of a mackerel fish sky and I call it halal sky *the eat any fish that has scales sky,* a kosher sky.

The Talmud itself says for a fish to be declared kosher scales and fins must be visible to the eye just like here a tastiest a super-fresh fish flashing its scales a good Christian sky for Leviticus (11:9–10) states that one should eat "whatsoever hath fins and scales in the waters" but not to eat "all that have not fins and scales in the seas." Rubin says that this means that fish with scales are intended to be eaten, such as salmon and trout, but smooth fish such as catfish and eels should not be eaten. but please let us have our big fish dinners with those mussels, shrimps and clam bakes—

Three Precipitating Clouds

The cumulonimbus, the grandpa of this family throws hailstones from pea size to golf balls to baseballs banging down hard with its top of the cloud flattening as it reaches the stratosphere 65,000 feet up into the atmosphere looking like a cloud table as it tries too hard to spread laterally making continuous rain tin ton roof tops, breathy tintinnabulary tinkling beats a trimbrelled hollering a crackly or fap fap fapping of melodies of pink sounds of rain tapping on window noise. The nimbostratus, a mid-level cloud enjoys giving us continuous rain and snow falls into snowy scenes seen on vintage Christmas greeting cards with snow over rooftops scenes with gilded trees, church, small town & Victoria Santa Claus with prayer by the nativity or a white New York City snow falls on 5th Avenue then that long lasting dramatic cirrus filaments, slender threadlike or thick yarn fuzz and eastward-moving tufts producing localized heavy rain showers the cirrus an upper cloud shades and hues resembling cowlicks, locks, tresses of delicate hair or fancy commas in extravagant persian calligraphy those right to left farsi fonts with dots and full stops written in white gold makes you think of Mesopotamian ancient Near East across all the sky in wispy thick and thin lines of cirrus silky streams curling ice crystals falling-precipitate evaporating in the air midway before reaching a photo sphere of a wrap-around-wide-angle view eyes capturing the panorama a full-sphere sweep from right to left

photo by emir@parrotta, Barcelona, Spain

stunning outdoor art & architecture

Beautiful & dramatic Thunderclouds tall & imposing shapes growing vertically called cumulonimbus—a cumulus a heaped and nimbus a rain-storm is dense, towering vertical cloud, a powerful upward air currents' cylindrical monument a ziggurat reaching heaven a Nebuchadnezzar apocalypse of the Towers of Babel expressing human aspiration ambi-tion of idealistic dreams overreaching themselves growing up out of the ground up Roman columns purely a decorative Doric, ionic, Corinthian a Tuscan a stylized interpretation of a tree. TALL, straight, slender the Ro-man columns' cloud towers textured shaped and shadows mushrooming into thunderheads blooming like at Park Guell in Barcelona designed by Gaudi's living outdoor art structures broken through the earth's ground always against the mutable clouds~~always changing that never the same that transient impermanence

photo by cristina-gottardi-khX7PV12lno-unsplash (1).jpg

a cumulus to great heights

its towers growing upwardly into piles and bunches of garlands with like long stems effortlessly styled creative arrangements in different shapes and styles, the nosegay, posy, or tussie-mussie small flower bouquet like crescents, and those cascading whites with the wind, the *Mandolin Players and their Performances,* solo strumming down strokes on hidden strings with hidden fingers as the wind carries the white posies oscillating them like trendy Italian women wearing dresses and stilettos, formal, sexy sitting on Lambretta two-wheeler scooters effortlessly stylish, beautiful a relaxed fashionable and those pretty Asian tourists wearing in golden *ao dais* smiling from slow-moving pale white e-*scooters* a procession of a moving gathering so radiant and o-o-o-o-n fistfuls of white lily of the valley a floating bouquet sky a delicate texture of the bashful blooming atmosphere with that and a passing tight circular flock of white-winged seagulls skimming the cumulus clouds' loftiest skies

Unusual Cloud Formations

photo by the national oceanic and atmospheric administration
photo library on unsplash

the flying-saucer cloud

hovering the steep, of the Grand Canyon in Arizona, US
where top heavy rivers and dessert plants the Crimson Monkeyflowers
bloom in a variety of colors growing thick along the water's edge of the
Grand Canyon   red wall-stained and yellowish-gray and brownish-gray
cliffs, thick-bedded . . . rock layers of limestone
where butterflies and hummingbirds and bees closest to the reds and or-
anges those globemallow on steep slopes grow along the river among the
sacred datura flowers,
the moonflowers, who blooms white in the night with long extended pro-
boscises making it hard to not think of Georgia O'Keeffe.
Thunder River falls where mist   of the
cascading where its soaking flows into curving mountain silhouettes over
knoll, the peak's waves with downslope winds dipping into the lee-side
(lows) of the lee-ward sides' of cyclones' elevated terrainy mountain sides
impersonating those bowed contours of the mountains that UFO-
lenticularis just like the standing waves in rapids
right behind a boulder huge
in currents of a hurtling streams with waves and downslopes'
moist air streams gracefully into the
altocumulus lenticularis clouds standing still
no blowing downwindly   but stays
floating right above

the psychedelic-colored canyon walls, the rivers chocolaty at the bottom
of the gorge moving silently like veins,

and above that great collection of the brightly clusters of buds and brush
the flora and fauna of the Grand Canyon

Lenticularis

Observing downwards to the top of the Cumulus congestus Clouds
Looking from above down the brilliantly white cumulus congestus clouds,
sunlit networks of I see churches with steeples of the elaborate hierarchy
with the pope as head of the Roman Catholic Church the supreme power
held tremendous political power here its remnants visiting us in a cloud.
chimneys and towers strongly
shaded projections and lots of arches and domes like seeing down onto
Rome and look to the right and see parts of Hadrian's Pantheon columned
porch of 8 massive granite
Corinthian columns in front, two groups of four behind the Pantheon's
dome.
Or I can actually see Brooklyn Botanic Gardens looking
down from above and seeing trees of Japanese Cherry Blossoms esplanade
still in full bloom and see large broccoli
and cauliflowers plants everywhere and gorgeous!
Put on Beethoven or Nils Frahm, the neo-classical composer while watch-
ing these cloud builders piling higher & higher inside of cumulus conges-
tus clouds swirling air on warmth and moisture these clouds grow tall to
heights of 20,000 feet (6,000 meters) can almost imagine Dubai's silvery
and coppery gleam with sprouting camels among from the desert sand
dunes I see looking down from above.
Can you see New York City and Hong Kong's skyscapes at night with those
so sparkly Milky-Way Stars?

~

Contrails photo by dailia giandeini on unsplash

Contrails

on a boardwalk of slanted wooden planks with wafts of popcorn with melt-
ed butter, the knishes, Coppertone & cotton candy and the banner planes
ousted on beaches with Ariel advertising media
colorful airplanes pulling banners unmuffled, horns, and loudspeakers
buzzing along the coastline beaches with tails of smoky unusual clouds
always with the sun in the background those contrails

contrail shadows photo by michael-jasmund-LKTVwhoComF8-on unsplash

Contrail shadows

See black beams or dark lines stiffened rods in the sky
like snakes looking like canes in a creek
against the sun low
an airplane's exhaust
aerosols and water vapor & particles
then ice crystals bright
contrails shadows itself luminously lit
with a dark slab of tail behind it
The setting sun & a vertical exhaust trail
pointing past the full moon especially close to the earth
casting shadows appear to the right
of the line between the contrail itself
and the eye

down from nyc skyphoto by phil-hauser-qUAl6pjpKWA-unsplash.jpg

Looking Down from a New York City Sky

A Moving Macy's Thanksgiving Parade
clouded over and over
the sun comes out from behind.
Billowy, oh cirrocumulus dewy,
a grayness haze,
a lowering misty rises like night into the brume
it's that somewhere over after
the sunlight is still shinning though
there's twelve white clouds
above my house
outside the windowsills.
How they hover
how they coast
with Paddington Bear
I love the most.
There's Winnie, Baloo,
Yogi and and Snoopy
and Charlie Brown and Woodstock too.
Boris Badenov still trying to eliminate Rocky & Bull Winkle,
and do you remember Bud Abbott and Lou Costello?
That duo that "I'm a b-a-a-a-a-d boy!
And Who's on First?
Lookie look at bobo the hobo,
and teddy bear's floating.
Felix and Donald, and Elsie the cow
with the Marching Tin Soldier balloons.
So all swanky
big swaggering
with sun and moon
all always crossing my sky.

undulatus asperatus

a weirder and wonderfuller new category of cloud
though you can look down on the clouds inside the sidewalk puddle like
here between the garden and the curb by the hydrant and the parking sign
pole a more marvelous most chaotic & most turbulent patterns of furrow
with rows of harrowing ridges with undulating reels with spools bobbing
rippling the swelling more enhanced a haughtiness blu a roughest frantic
a sea choppiest most remarkable in a hot summer sidewalk this cement
puddle serenades of flashes of silvery whites and dusty grays and ash most
surely unforgiving but don't spill in don't sink in its conduit whatever you
do do, do not glimpse that glance upwardly cause it is a bad terrifying

a sea serpent cloud

of ice crystals that just don't dissipate it glides accordion stretches out pulling the rear part forward   extending in a continuous icy trail of ssssssssssserpentine stream of wind arrangement this rippled physique of a free-swimming umbrella-shaped bells and trailing tentacles this Jelly fish snakes sways with its head an Altocumulus lenticularis

a right to left over that mountain peak poking its tongue out hissing heavily up there propelling into an 'S' shape bending it spine into serpentine coils volutes or twists grips using the curves to push across the sidewinding that side to side motion that locomotion wriggling. a quick writhing, a jutting out from the sky bank in frigid air

celestial trilobite

fossils
made up of sand,
silt, mud
the most efficacious of all early animals,
existing for almost 300 million years
found in mountains,
in deserts on cliffs and right here high
above in clouds,
a floating in our sky.
That giant celestial trilobite
the wind carries it
like a parcel of cloudy air,
across our always-moving atmosphere.
Now hurries over head
that tattered symmetry
sailing white
delicate filaments
threadlike Cirrus
squished flattened
fossilized long,
streamer like tail feathers
a starling's rainbow sheen
a peacock's glittering tail
or from spectacular ancient birds or even from
from feathered dinosaur
floating fossils
astoundingly gorgeous
threadbare rocks aloft on air

billow clouds

These clouds really make waves so wavy like sea sandbars'small rip currents flow between breaks in the swirling turbulence of flouting off beach excavates a trough's sandy bottom's banks beneath a shallow sea organized in mostly parallel rows like how these variations of the undulatus when wind gusts at varying speeds looking like whitecaps coil with a deep rise and slow fall—darker cloud patterns in the background curls, surges, gush swells turbulent blows looking up into our middle or low atmosphere

Mammatus Clouds

rare & beautiful
the mammatus clouds
underneath anvil clouds
udder-like shapes
rain-filled sacks
take a surreal moment
as the sun goes down
those pinks blues orange hues
sunset skyscapes
just after the worst
of worst of thunderstorms have passed
floating voluptuous clouds in sinking air
some bell shapes with gentler slops
there a asymmetric heavier
narrower at the top
that drastically fuller
towards the bottom
one round
boobs to bras
those equally full
enlarged breasts without nipples
Venus of pendulous breasts
orifices abstracted & rearranged
irregularly shaped
sagging pomegranates
from our fruit-bearing
our deciduous sky shrubs
from wonderful cherry & plum tree too
blossoms in its dainty flowers
full bloom
revered blossoming trees
floating along the flanks of thunderstorms

Ode to NASA Hubble Space Telescope

massive interstellar rises among the multitude parallel universes hot beds
of stellar evolution beautiful blue nebula billowing towers rising cloud of
dust from Eagle, the stellar nursery,
bright and dark swimming in dark caves the complex nebulosity like a stem
in a rosebud
in our constellation. Cloud of dust and gas 7,500 light-years from EARTH,
this interstellar cloud. Mystic Mountain, full of spires of foxgloves back row
of plant beds the dark flowers with veitch's blue small globe thistles like a
parallel universe sparkly star cluster cloud thinly spread interstellar gas &
dust Celestial structures assemblies seen in NASA Hubble Space Telescope
a tapering conical a pyramidal structure like on the top of a building a
carved church tower vast pillar-like structures. The spires & columns of
Carina Nebula crumble and a close encounter with a giraffe scoping out for
cassava leaves its neck in a lazy curvy kind of curl.

prague clouds and telephone poles photo by parrotta.emile@gmail.com

dear emile,

even though I am far away
here in Virginia, USA
and you in Prague over that pond there far
those Utility poles supporting overhead powerlines
& electrical wires
& cables delivering landline telephone
and digital DSL radius is on poles
above the ground other conduits, cables
& wires strung
in air in a curtain of coaxial cables
range from submarine fiber optic cables
through to mobile phone mast
on towards data centers
& telephone exchanges
on your street to your house to mine
amaze us
against the all blue
& cloudy clouds' definite decorative lines
Creating balance & mindfulness
a place where we meet
through those silky sheens of white cirrus,
wispy ice streamers
or inside the developing towers
of the cumulus always initiating lifts
such as over barriers of hills,
mountains or above
all the distances
 farther away
between us our cloud photographs
of our global consciousness
connect from swirls of white glowing

with sunlight or darken
with rain from your everyday to mine
there our shared sky
above our heads
resembling recumbent rivers passing over land

www.ingramcontent.com/pod-product-compliance
Lightning Source LLC
Chambersburg PA
CBHW071110090426
42737CB00013B/2552